SILAS
and the
MAd-SAD
PEOPLE

written by amber jayanti
illustrated by ellen beier

NEW SEED PRESS
P.O. Box 3016
Stanford, CA 94305
copyright © 1981

ISBN 0-938678-08-6

Library of Congress Catalog Card No: 80–83882

PRESS
1944 UNIVERSITY AVE.
E. PALO ALTO, CA. 94303
TEL: 328-3944

To my dear son, Zeek Silver Moon

SPAGHETTI SOUP

It was getting to be suppertime on a winter's afternoon. Silas Rain Rivers posted a "No Trespassing" sign on the door to his room and carefully closed himself in. Silas loved his room and all the stuff in it. Papier-mâché masks stuck out on the walls, his trombone stood ready against his bed, and cars of all sizes peeked out of the corners. Sometimes his mom and dad said funny things about his room.

"Silas, you must need a road map to find your shoes," his dad would joke.

Mom would stick her head in at bedtime and call, "Please light my way, Silas, so I don't get nibbled on by the floor."

This afternoon Silas sat busily at his workbench. It's just perfect, he decided, brushing the final strokes of silver paint on his very first model airplane. Silas's stomach rumbled as he listened to his parents fixing supper in the kitchen.

"Yumm, spaghetti soup," whispered Silas, sniffing the soupy air stealing under his door. "And it's so nice they have stopped fighting for a while."

But suddenly his mom's and dad's voices grew louder and louder. "I hate this," Silas groaned, tossing his paintbrush down. Then came a big *crash*!

"I'm getting out of here right now!" yelled his dad.

"Don't hurry back!" his mom shouted.

Slam went the porch door. He heard the car start and with a great speed rush away. Silas slumped over his very first model airplane holding his ears. There was so much unhappiness in the house these days. Silas could hardly remember how good it felt to fall asleep to the sound of his dad's piano playing and his mom's singing.

Silas's heart pounded as he crept toward the kitchen.

"Oh, Mom!" he gasped, standing in the doorway.

Spaghetti soup ran down the wall where his school pictures hung. His mom sat bent over in Grandpa's rocker.

"Oh, Silas," she choked out, "I felt like Dad was ordering me around, and I got so angry that I smashed the Tiger."

The Tiger Bowl lay in a corner on the blue tile floor. Steamy soup slowly dribbled through its cracked places.

"My bowl, my very favorite one!" Silas cried out.

Silas's mom got up to hug him close, but his small body stiffened.

"Noah's mom made it especially for my birthday. I am mad at you for breaking it! I am mad at you for wrecking my pictures! I am mad at you and Dad for fighting!" he yelled angrily.

"I'm really sorry," Mom said. "Dad and I seem to be arguing over almost everything. Most of the time we

6

don't even know how it gets started." She wiped her face with a soup-stained hand and sighed, "But what I do know is that we're all sure getting hurt a lot."

"Yeah, Mom, it hurts." Silas shivered into her shoulder.

THE MAD-SAD PEOPLE

Silas secretly named his mom and dad, the *mad-sad people*. He loved his parents no matter what, but lately he hardly knew who they were. Mom seemed to snap more than the curly old dog across the street. Her mouth still smiled when Silas made his silly faces, but not her eyes. She grew thinner and paler each day, looking more and more like a leftover Halloween witch. Dad stopped playing his piano. He said he was too tired to run with Silas and their pup, Bell, before dinner. His face was so dark and tearful that it hurt Silas to look at him.

Mealtime was silent, and even the food tasted mad. "Everybody-on-the-couch for hug-time," disappeared. Nobody came to visit and sing by the fire. Breakfasts were lonely without Dad's "good-morning story," and there were no more of Mom's homemade breads.

Yes, thought Silas, living with the *mad-sad people* is terrible for me!

Many nights Silas couldn't fall asleep. He tossed about in his bed disturbed by the muffled arguments in the room upstairs. "I wish they would stop it!" he said over and over to himself. Things seemed to be getting worse and worse. Then came the night Dad shouted, "I am going to find a new place to live!" Mom began shouting back and crying at the same time. Silas wanted to run to them calling, "No! No! Stop it!" but his body stuck to the bed.

If only I could do something to help, he thought.

"Maybe if I wasn't here everything would be all right again," he mumbled as he began to cry.

That night Silas dreamed he ran away to a city where children stayed until their moms and dads became happy again. Large red letters on its entrance gate warned: NO MAD-SAD PEOPLE ALLOWED.

THE WORLD'S BEST BUDDIES

Saturday's sunshine streaked through Silas's bedroom window. Silas peeped through one eye and pulled the covers back over his head. After overhearing the night before that his dad was leaving, the sun felt like rain. Then he remembered it was Saturday. He pushed off his quilts and poked his head under the bed.

"Hey, Bell," he called, "it's Saturday and we're going to visit Noah and Chuff."

Bell gave a gigantic yawn as she stretched her fuzzy front legs. Since Mom and Dad already knew of his plan, he left without waking them.

Silas ran beside his red, white, and blue two-wheeler down the sidewalk as Bell pranced eagerly behind him. Barely stopping, he swung one leg over the crossbar. He hunched his back, gripped the handlebars, and began making long, loud motor-like sounds. *"Vrooom! Vrooom! Vroooom!"* Bell yowled along. Silas cleared his throat. "This will be a six-block race," he announced to Bell. "Ready . . . go!" Helped by a strong gust of wind, the pair was off to a speedy start.

Mail carriers and newspaper trucks moved about the slowly awakening neighborhood. Here and there, a few folks waited at their windows for Saturday's morning paper. Nearing Alice's Bicycle Shop, Silas saw the small woman in overalls rolling tires through her side door. Silas beeped his horn. Alice waved a tire in return.

"Hey, where are you two going so early?" she called to them.

"To our Best Buddy's house," Silas answered, without stopping.

Two more blocks, thought Silas, rounding the corner. He started peddling faster and faster, thinking, I bet

11

Noah will go all through school with me just the way Matthew did with Dad. Yes, Noah and I really are the world's best buddies.

THE BROKEN RULE

From the time Silas began playing with other children, he was taught a very important rule: *talk before you hit, and if that doesn't work, get help!*

"Tie!" yelled Silas as he and Bell skidded into Noah and Chuff's driveway. Wiggling with excitement, Chuff bounded through the toy-scattered yard to greet his visitors. After a joyful exchange of scents, the pups dashed under the house, and Silas sprinted the back steps two at a time. Silas loved pancakes, but the sight of Noah's family happily gathered for breakfast made his appetite vanish.

"You must have smelled them five blocks away," Noah's dad teased, flipping a hot pancake past his nose.

"There are hundreds of them," cheered Noah, getting out another plate.

"No, thanks, I'm not hungry," Silas admitted, backing away from the table. "I'll meet you in your room when you're done."

Everyone looked surprised as he quickly headed

13

toward Noah's room.

With a churning stomach, Silas closed the door. "I don't really want to be here. I don't really want to be home. But where can I go?" he asked himself, dropping face down onto the loopy orange rug. Soon Noah came humming down the hall. Silas sat up and crossed his legs.

"Let's play checkers," Noah greeted him.

"O.K," Silas agreed half-heartedly.

As the boys played, Silas kept thinking about his dad finding another place to live. Suddenly he found himself losing, and he definitely didn't like it. So when his next turn came, Silas stole two moves.

"I saw that!" cried Noah.

"Saw what?" asked Silas, trying hard not to look guilty.

"You took two moves!" Noah hissed.

Silas turned very pink. Noah stood up and flipped the checkerboard over.

"Cheaters lose automatically," Noah said. "The game is over and I'm the winner!"

Then Silas broke The Rule.

"You are not!" he yelled, punching Noah hard in the ribs.

Noah began to cry. "Go home, Silas, you aren't my friend anymore!"

Silas felt sorry but couldn't let the words come out.

14

"I'd better get out of here," Silas said, running for his bike. He disappeared so fast that Bell almost got left behind.

THE EXPERIMENT

Hot and panting, Silas and Bell burst through the open porch door. Mom and Dad lay sprawled out on the couch listening to the radio. Looking at them, Silas thought, I'd like to hit and hug them at the same time. But instead, he kicked Bell so hard that she slid into the fireplace, tail first. Then she ran whimpering under the kitchen table, her creamy fur streaked with ashes.

His parents sat up as if jolted by electricity and immediately snapped off the radio.

"Silas, I want to know exactly why you hurt Bell?" Dad demanded.

Silas puffed out his chest, squinted, pushed out his bottom lip and said, "Because I wanted to! I'm mad at her! She's a stupid dog and I hate her!"

Although Silas's body resisted, Dad gently pulled him onto the couch.

"We definitely know how it feels to be mad," Dad said.

"It must be hard for you to live with us when we

15

fight and are angry most of the time," Mom said.

Silas clenched his fists and exclaimed in his loudest voice, "It's horrible! Terrible! Miserable!"

Mom nodded. "Well, it has been that way for us, too."

Dad rubbed Silas's sweaty head and whispered sadly, "We are so very, very sorry."

"We honestly want it to be different now," Mom continued, "so Dad and I are going to try an experiment."

"What kind of experiment?" grumbled Silas.

Dad took a long deep breath, and said, "I'm going to move to another house."

"I don't want you to do that!" Silas said. "I want it to be like it used to be. Why can't it be like that again?"

Dad took another deep breath. "Hard as it may be to understand, I'm learning that things never really stay the same. Everything is always growing and changing, people, plants and animals."

"I don't care," wailed Silas, "I want it to be the same!"

Dad's face drooped. "Yes, I know how you feel. Sometimes I do, too. Changes do make things different at first, but they are as much a part of the world as the sun and the rain."

"Why Silas," his mom said, "if you didn't grow and

17

change you wouldn't be able to ride your bike, or talk, or play the trombone. In fact, you would still be wearing diapers."

Silas nearly smiled at the thought of himself in diapers. Slowly Mom's face brightened. "When I was your age, Grandpa George told me, 'If life feels so bad that it just can't be any worse, it *must* be ready to change and get better.'"

"Oh," sniffled Silas, remembering his grandpa's sparkling eyes and wonderful hugs. And then he thought, maybe this experiment will be the end of the *mad-sad people*. It sure is time for that!

SILAS IS FIRST

Over the next few weeks, Silas pretended not to notice the full trash cans and growing piles of books, records, and knickknacks on the floor of his dad's music room. But then came the drizzly afternoon at school when Silas understood that his dad really was going to move. Silas was waiting in his yellow rain slicker under an enormous oak tree when his dad's station wagon pulled up.

"You look just like a big wet mushroom waiting to be picked," Dad greeted him. "And you know how much

I love mushrooms."

Silas's whole face smiled. "I love you, Dad Mushroom," he answered as he dropped his lunch pail into the car. But his bright smile vanished the second he caught sight of some over-stuffed boxes piled into the back of the car.

"Are you starting to move already?" he asked.

"Yes, and today *we* are going to visit my new house."

Silas pictured his own house very empty without his dad. "Ow, my leg hurts 'cause I fell off my bike yesterday," he said. "Let's go next week."

"So your leg hurts and you want to go next week," Dad repeated, patting Silas's leg gently. "I don't feel so good myself. With all this packing and moving, my feelings are sure hurting a lot. But, Silas, since it's going to be your sometime-home, I really wanted you to be the first to see it."

Silas hung his head down to his chest. After a long, quiet time, he looked up right into his dad's eyes and asked, "Before your Best Buddy Matthew?"

"Most definitely!" Dad said. "Besides," he added, pointing at the boxes, "I'd look very funny driving around with all these for the next week."

"O.K. Let's go," Silas agreed, buckling his seat belt for the ride.

"Here we are," Dad announced as the car stopped by a curly, wrought-iron gate.

Pigeons sat on its top. Away they flew as Silas pushed it open. A tall, lemon yellow house with three colored-glass windows and a chocolate brown roof reached for the sky. Silas thought, It almost looks like a birthday cake, and he licked his lips.

"Is this big house all yours, Dad?" he asked, zig-zagging his way to the front door.

"No, David and Doug live here, too," Dad explained as he fitted his key into the flower-curtained front door. "They have the downstairs and we'll have the upstairs."

The hall smelled of freshly baked cookies. Silas's stomach gurgled.

"Anybody home?" Dad's voice echoed.

"Just follow your nose," a deep voice answered.

Silas easily sniffed his way into the sweet-smelling kitchen.

"Hi, I'm David," said a red-faced man just closing the oven door. "You're right on time!" He held out two still-warm cookies to Silas's waiting hands.

"Thanks. Oatmeal-raisin are my favorite," Silas managed to say between bites.

Another man in a bright blue shirt sat at the table

sipping tea. "I'm Doug," he said from behind his steaming mug. "You must be Lanny's son, Hungry."

Silas laughed cookie crumbs from the corners of his mouth.

"I am Silas Rain Rivers," he answered, standing very tall, "and I came to see my sometime-place."

Dad walked to the far corner of the kitchen and pulled on a snaky rope that was hanging from the ceiling. As if by some magician's trick, out slipped a long wooden ladder.

"Let's climb it," he said to Silas.

Silas's eyes and mouth opened wide. I can't wait till Noah sees this, thought Silas, as he began to climb. But suddenly Silas felt sad all over when he remembered that he hadn't played with Noah since their fight many weeks ago.

HOW THE SPIDER PLANT WAS SAVED

As Silas crawled over the ladder top, a large, funny-shaped room appeared. Light streamed through a colored-glass window and a mobile of sea shells tinkled overhead. The walls and ceilings were old, golden grained wood.

Silas became so interested in everything that he didn't notice his dad's disappearing around a corner.

"Silas, come and see *this*," Dad called, poking out his head. Silas quickly followed.

Surrounded by a curtain printed with planets and space creatures was a low, comfortable-looking bed and a round table with two chairs, all exactly Silas's size. In the center of the table lay a miniature ready-to-be-assembled rocketship.

Dad looked proud and said, "I sewed the curtain and built the bed myself. And I thought you could help me build the rocketship."

Silas silently chewed his bottom lip.

"Well, how do you like it?" Dad asked.

Silas shrugged his shoulders up to his ears. "It's all right, I guess, but it's not as nice as *my* house." Silas felt like crying.

Dad sank to his knees before Silas. "Yes, you definitely know *your* house a lot better than this one. But, Silas, the thing about experiments is they can lead to some very new places."

Silas blinked tears from his eyes.

"Your mom and I need to live apart right now," Dad said, "and that is not an easy idea to get used to. We're all going to miss some of the things we shared."

Still crying, Silas nodded his head.

"I was just thinking back to last summer," Dad said, softly, "when your Spider plant started dying. Nothing we

25

tried helped it. Then we took it over to Molly's Plant Shop and were told that in order to save it we must divide and repot it as two smaller plants. Well, Mom and I feel just like that plant right now — only people grow better in houses than in pots."

Silas leaned over, hugged his dad, and closed his eyes. He remembered how he and Dad had divided and repotted the Spider, and how surprised he was when the separation brought the two plants to life again.

Suddenly Silas had an idea. "Dad," he whispered excitedly, "will you please take one of the Spider plants to *this* house?"

Dad gave him a loving pinch. "You know, Silas, I was just thinking the same exact thing!"

MOVING DAY AND SOME SURPRISE VISITORS

Everybody moved on the first day of Spring.

"Now Silas, call me whenever you feel like it," Dad said as they exchanged telephone numbers.

Silas looked serious and said, "That's a deal. And you call me, too."

The whole family, including one Spider plant, gathered in the driveway for a Goodbye-till-Sunday-hug. Silas felt better knowing that he would be spending

Sundays and one night during the week with his dad. His parents had also assured him that the experiment had not cancelled out his Easter vacation with Grandma Florence.

Mom's face became very thoughtful. "The first part of our experiment feels over to me," she said, "and I do believe we've all done very well."

Silas and Dad nodded and Silas thought, This is the best hug in a long, long time. He was happily squished between Mom, Dad and Bell.

Later that morning Mom showed Silas the calendar. "Today is the beginning of Spring, which means the start of new life." Silas was interested. "It also is a fine time for moving, housecleaning and throwing away old possessions," she said. Silas frowned.

"Dad sure threw away a lot of stuff before he moved," Silas said.

Mom stroked his head. "Yes, he did, and I need to do the very same thing."

Silas grew quiet, but after a minute, he shouted, "Mom, I wish we'd move my bed onto the porch so my room can be just for playing. Then I'd have *two* new houses."

"Great idea," she answered, turning in that direction.

"I'll carry the quilts and pillows," he volunteered, following close behind her.

The record player sang as they worked. Silas danced

with Bell. A few times he found his mom singing, dancing, crying, and cleaning all at the same time!

"How can you do all of that together?" he asked her.

"Because I am feeling both happy and sad at the same time," she answered, leaning over to whisk some dust from his hair.

By the time the last trash can was emptied, the sun had set and stomachs were calling for food. As Mom turned out the supper rolls for kneading, the doorbell rang. Tired, and already in his pajamas, Silas answered it. There on the front steps stood Noah, his mom, and Chuff. Noah smiled shyly as he held out his hand.

"Hi, Silas. I want to shake and be friends again, O.K.?"

Silas smiled, too, and held out his hand. "I'm sorry for hitting you and being a cheater," he said. By the time the boys had finished shaking hands, both moms were laughing and Chuff and Bell raced happily to the back yard.

There was supper to share and a warm fire to sit by. Dinner was a mixture of good feelings and delicious food: vegetables on long forks roasted in the fireplace, buttery rolls, hot cocoa, and for desert, Silas's favorite — banana ice cream. After the last bite had been eaten, Noah, his mom and Chuff sleepily headed home.

A VERY SPECIAL LOVE PLACE

How perfectly my bed fits under the window, thought Silas as he showed Bell her new place. Lying down, Silas could see the stars shimmering in the cool, dark air.

Mom came in carrying an extra quilt.

"I thought you and Dad were all grown-up," he said as she arranged the quilt over him.

Mom flopped down on the bed beside him. "I used to think so, too," she said, "but I'm slowly learning that even though people may look grown on the outside, they still aren't finished growing up on the inside."

Silas looked worried. "Are you and Dad going to grow not to love me?" His voice trembled.

Mom took his hands gently in hers. "So you are afraid that we will stop loving you?" Silas tightly squeezed her hands.

"Well," she said, "it's definitely time to tell you an important fact. When children are born, a very special love place is born in the hearts of their moms and dads. It's so special that it's *always* there, even though they may not be together all of the time."

"Can children have a place like that for moms and dads?" he asked.

"They sure can!" she answered, smiling her most beautiful smile.

31

"Oh. . . . !" breathed Silas.

They sat for what seemed like forever watching the moonlight fill the sky. Silas yawned sleepily when his mom got up and stretched. "Good night little snuggle-mouse. I love you," she whispered, planting a kiss on the tip of his nose.

"I love you, too. . . and Dad," he muttered into his pillow.

That night Silas Rain Rivers dreamed he saw the very special love place inside himself and watched it as it grew bigger and bigger and bigger!